Table of Contents

ADVANCED
COMMUNICATION S

WHY IS IT SO IMPORTANT TO COMMUNI
THAT WILL MAKE YOU AN EFFECTIVE COM.

MATTHEW RICHARDSO

INTRODUCTION

---- ✲ ----

WHY ARE COMMUNICATION SKILLS IMPORTANT?

You have taken the most important step on the road to becoming a master communicator. Every effort was made to ensure this book is full of as much useful information as possible. Please enjoy!

Why are communication skills important?

That's a fair question. We hear about how important communication is everywhere. But how can you tell the contenders from the pretenders? There are many self-proclaimed experts out there, but very few actually deliver the goods.

So, you've come to the right place.

This book will take a deep look into communication, it's importance, and why the basics of communication skills aren't enough to make you successful in today's demanding world. People all over, in churches, offices, factories, clubs and at home, need to use communication skills to get along with everyone around them.

Successful communicators know the skills needed to get their message across and elicit the proper response from the interlocutors. The good news is that these skills can all be learned. If effective communicators can learn these skills, then so can you.

Now, let's roll up our sleeves and get started!

Why Communication Is Important

Any human interaction involves communication-that simple. In business, professionals needed to achieve effective communication with superiors, subordinates, suppliers, and most importantly, clients. By taking a closer look at some of the most effective executives in business, you can detect a pattern in how effective communication can be mastered.

Now, one thing is being an effective communicator by mastering basic communication skills, and it is an entirely different thing to be a master communicator. You can master this art form by learning, and practicing, advanced communication skills. It not only takes time and practice, but it also requires the desire, motivation, and skills that most ordinary people simply don't have.

Effective communication is an art that demands practice and an advanced skill set.

Effective communication is essential not just in the business world, but anywhere in life. Can you think of any place where you don't need effective communication? Unless you are a hermit living on a mountaintop, you will need to be an effective communicator anywhere you go.

Most people understand that communication skills are an essential asset to developing their careers. Yet, so few are willing to put in the work needed to learn the basic, not to mention the advanced skills required to truly excel in the workplace. Those that struggle to get their ideas, message, and intentions across, will find it rather hard to achieve their full potential. After all, could you pitch your business ideas to investors without strong communication skills?

But as I mentioned, communication skills are there for anyone to learn. Often, all you need is a push in the right direction. By looking into the basics of communication, you can unlock many opportunities around you. By mastering advanced communication skills, you can reel in opportunities you never thought possible!

What sets advanced communication skills apart from basic communication skills?

How could you define communication? Think about it for a moment... most folks would consider communication to be a verbal process in which two individuals exchange information through language, be it written or spoken. Frankly, that falls flat.

Communication is an artistic process by which people create and share ideas. Effective communication is built upon the ease with which these ideas are transmitted.

So, basic communication skills focus on being able to get your message across in a way that anyone can understand it. The basics are framed within a process that is usually enabled by language. When individuals do not speak the same language, communication breaks down. Even when individuals talk the same language, but lack the proper skills, communication cannot take place.

Upon getting a handle on the basics, advanced skills take communication to a whole new level. In essence, advanced communication skills are leadership skills wrapped in your own, personal way of doing things. After all, how could you be an effective leader if you cannot communicate?

Have you ever had a boss that was simply unable to inspire and motivate you? Then you know exactly how vital communication skills can be.

What exactly do we mean by "Advanced Communication Skills"?

In this book, we'll be taking an in-depth look at the basics of communication, and then we'll sink our teeth into advanced communication skills. Think of the basics as the rungs on the ladder on our way to effective communication.

Once we've covered the basics, then we'll focus on the following skills:

- How the communication process works. We'll be looking at the different types of input, the filters with which we "map out" the information we receive in our minds and how these filters can influence what we understand.

- How we perceive the information we have received. This perception depends on the means with which we receive the information we get. For example, there are visual means, auditory means, and so on.

- Rapport building. Which is a desired skill that so few can manage. We'll take a look at a simple, five-stage process in which we'll discover how we can build rapport with those around us.

- The toolbox. Just like any good artist, we'll develop a toolbox that you can take with you anywhere you go. This toolbox contains a variety of strategies which you can put to use to home in on your objectives and take your communication skills to the next level.

I don't know about you, but I'm excited to be going down this path. Like you, I wasn't always the best communicator, but I learned, and through experience, I was able to learn the advanced communication skills that have helped me to achieve my personal and professional objectives.

Thanks to advanced communication skills, I was able to get ahead in my career, have fulfilling personal relationships, and get whatever I wanted just because I could ask the right questions and elicit the right responses from the right people.

If I can do it, so can you!

So, what are you waiting for? Let's jump right in and get started with some communication basics.

CHAPTER 1

─── ≋ ───

COMMUNICATION BASICS

Picture this: you're part of a space exploration mission to a new planet. Suddenly, the ship has an engine failure, and you are forced to land on an unknown planet. Then, your ship is surrounded by a creature you have never seen before. It seems like they are talking, and they seem non-threatening, but you can't understand a word they are saying. They are trying to tell you something, but they don't speak your language either. How can you possibly communicate with them?

I know, this example seems a bit extreme, but doesn't it feel like you're on a different planet when you can't communicate with others? I know, I've been there. And while the people around you are not from another planet, if you can't communicate effectively, they might as well be. That is why communication is so important.

When you are unable to communicate with someone, the hindrances, or barriers, which keep you from communicating, could be the result of differences in culture, age, personality, among many others. So, it is your task to break through these barriers, so that you can get your message across.

Depending on circumstances, you might encounter one barrier, or perhaps multiple barriers, at the same time. Effective communication uses tools to break down these barriers and get the message across. Many times, the first step to breaking through these barriers is to acknowledge that they are there first.

Naturally, communication is not one-sided; otherwise, it wouldn't be communication. Communication is a two-way phenomenon whereby both sides send messages back and forth. Of course, you can rely on your interlocutor's skills. But that may not always be effective. After all, what happens if your interlocutor lacks basic communication skills? But if you do, you can aid the other party to communicate with you.

Your skills can make up for your interlocutor's lack of skills. Picture a soccer match in which your partner is trying to pass you the ball. Ideally, both of you would run, and your partner would anticipate where you are. That way, your partner could send the ball straight to you. But what if your partner doesn't have the skills to find you? If you have the skills to find your partner, you can get open, so they can see you and pass you the ball. That often leads to goals.

The previous example is why sports metaphors are so successful in explaining how the dynamic of communication works. So, let's dig deeper into the nuts and bolts of this dynamic.

The Communication Dynamic

The communication dynamic is not static, but rather, totally dynamic. It can also be broken down into 8 phases:

1. Sender
2. Package
3. Encoding
4. Means
5. Recipient
6. Decoding
7. Feedback
8. Context

The following figure illustrates the way this dynamic works:

Figure 1

The Communication Dynamic

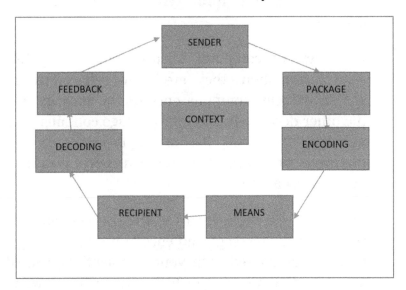

As you can see, the communication dynamic is a feedback loop in which the sender's encoded message, or package, reaches the intended recipient who then decodes the package and sends feedback to the sender. It's important to keep in mind that the means are the way in which we communicate, be it verbally or non-verbally. The successful outcome of this loop results in effective communication.

Now, let's take a closer look at each one of these elements:

1. **Sender.** The sender is the source of communication. For the purpose of this book, it is YOU. To be a good sender, you must be clear on what your message is, and most importantly, why you are sending it. What is it that you want to convey? Do you know who your recipient is? If you can't answer any of these questions, then you need to go back to the drawing board. **You must understand why you are communicating and what your intended outcome is.**

2. **Package.** In computer science, when computers send information, they are often referred to as "packages". One computer encodes the package, and the other decodes it. So, your package contains your message. Otherwise, it's an empty package. **The package contains the reason why you are communicating.**

3. **Encoding.** Essentially, this is the process whereby you take your message and encode it into a package that can be shared with your recipient. You must avoid sending a package which your recipient won't be able to open. That would lead to communication

breakdown. Your interlocutor must be able to decode your package. This is why you must consider the right package for your message. Can your recipient open it? Is this the best package for your message and your intended recipient? Are there any linguistic, cultural, or personal factors that you need to consider? **What would be the best package for someone with a visual or hearing disability?**

4. **Means**. The means is the way that you are going to send your package. The means for your package could be something as simple as a telephone call, or something highly complex like an encrypted message over a secure network. Modern technology has given us a plethora of means. For instance, we have Skype, FaceTime, chat, WhatsApp, email, social media, or any other means you can think of. And while each channel has its advantages and disadvantages, **you need to find the right one for your intended recipients.**

5. **Recipient.** This is your target. This is your audience. Once you have considered the right message, package, and means, you need to consider your recipient's expectations, beliefs, opinions, and perception. By taking into account your recipient's aims, you can improve the chances of your message getting through successfully. Your message needs to resonate with your recipient. For example, **if you're attempting to communicate with senior citizens, would an internet-based campaign be the best means to deliver your package?**

6. **Decoding.** Once your recipient gets the package, they need to figure out how to open it. This is where your communication skills play a crucial role. Your recipient needs to perceive, understand, process and internalize your message. If your recipient lacks the skills needed to decode your package, then you would either have to resend it through more appropriate means or aid your recipient in opening the package. **Think of how you could better explain yourself without using fancy vocabulary.**

7. **Feedback.** Once you have sent your package, it has been received and opened, feedback can determine if the communication dynamic was successful. For instance, if you are delivering a speech, you can judge if you are getting through to your audience by judging their reactions. This is how experienced teachers know if their students are getting it, or not. **Feedback is the means by which you can determine if your communication efforts were successful, or if they need to be improved.**

8. **Context.** This is the ever-present situation in which the communication dynamic takes place. Much of the process itself depends on the context. After all, you won't always communicate in the same place, at the same time and with the same people. For instance, your context could be the boardroom, a bar on a Friday night, the gym, or your home. **Effective communicators are able to tailor their communication skills to suit the occasion.**

Aspects of the Communication Dynamic

So, what do you need to do in order to communicate with others? How can we communicate without using words? As you gain a deeper understanding of communication, you will find that communication takes place without words. In traditional face-to-face communication, words, or verbal cues, are only part of the story. In fact, most of our message is conveyed through non-verbal means, such as body language, tone, intonation, gestures and so forth.

Figure 2

Aspects of the communication dynamic

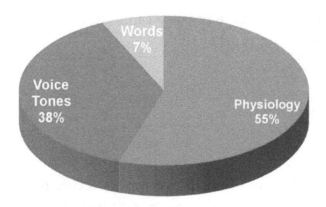

It is evident that verbal cues are only a part of the overall communication dynamic. Therefore, effective communicators are not just talking; they are able to manipulate their tone of voice and their non-verbal cues, such as body language, to suit the message they wish to convey.

Let's take a closer look at verbal and non-verbal communication.

Non-Verbal Communication

We tend to focus on verbal communication as the only way we convey meaning in a conversation. But this could not be further from the truth. It is said that 93% of our communication happens through non-verbal means. Think about that for a moment... aspects such as tone of voice and gestures can have a tremendous impact on the message you are trying to send. And even if your verbal communication is crystal clear, your non-verbal cues can derail your efforts.

For example, the tone of voice can have a powerful impact on the meaning of what you are saying. Take this sentence for example:

I love you

I **love** you

I love **you**

We all understand that "I love you" is a very nice thing to say. However, the bolded words indicate a different type of meaning. While the phrase is something nice to say to someone, by emphasizing "I" you are saying that it is "I" who loves you. Likewise, emphasizing "love" means that you want the other person to it is the love you are talking about. Lastly, the emphasis on "you" means that I love YOU and no one else. And while the phrase's meaning has not changed, the message can be very different.
Now, add in the right body language, such as a hug, and your message will surely hit the mark!

Here are some examples of body language:

- Facial gestures (expressions)
- Posture (the way we sit or stand)
- Swaying (moving back and forth)
- Hand gestures
- Eye contact
- Breathing
- Coughing
- Blushing
- Fidgeting

This list underscores some of the most common behaviors we can observe when attempting to communicate. Many times, we are not even aware we are exhibiting these behaviors. The following are good examples of how you don't need to say anything to communicate your feelings.

- Joe has got his arms crossed over his chest. His head in down and he is looking away from you. His fingers are tapping on his arm very quickly.

- Mary is sitting in her chair, comfortably back with her arms crossed behind her neck. She occasionally nods and smiles while you speak.

- Bob is leaning in very close to you. His voice is just above a whisper and in a hurried tone. He is making very swift gestures with his hands.

- Jenny is making a presentation to the sales team. She is constantly moving, she can't keep her hands still, and she is fidgeting with her hair.

- Jack is in a meeting. His legs are swinging very quickly. He has one hand on his chin, and the other is clicking a pen.

Without hearing a single word from these people, we can guess how they feel. That's how powerful non-verbal communication can be. Would you like to be seen like this?

Verbal Communication

It's Incredible when you think about the fact that verbal communication has the least impact in a conversation. While it is no less critical, verbal communication doesn't necessarily produce the same outcomes as non-verbal communication. In a way, "it's not what you say, but how you say it".

Now, it would be naïve to think that verbal communication does not play a significant role. Of course, it does. Saying the wrong thing at the wrong time can kill your career. Conversely, saying the right thing at the right time can boost your career to new heights. That's why it is so important to mind your words and not speak unless you are sure about what you are going to say.

In those times when we only have verbal communication, such as in a telephone call, it is of the utmost importance for you to have a game plan. You can't afford to "wing it", especially in an important call, since saying the wrong thing can have a lasting impact on a relationship or business deal.

So, maintaining a friendly tone throughout a conversation can go a long way toward getting ahead in business and life.

CHAPTER 2

---- ≋ ----

A CLOSER LOOK AT THE COMMUNICATION DYNAMIC

In the previous chapter, we grasped the basics on communication and its phases. In this chapter, we'll talk a closer look at the way communication works and how we can take advantage of that information and use it to improve our communication skills. We'll also be looking at how the brain processes the messages it received and how your own experiences impact your ability to communicate. We'll also have a look at how we can identify the filters that others have.

So, let's get started!

Types of Input

To kick things off, let's have a look at figure 3 which illustrates how the brain processes the input.

Figure 3

How the Brain Processes Input

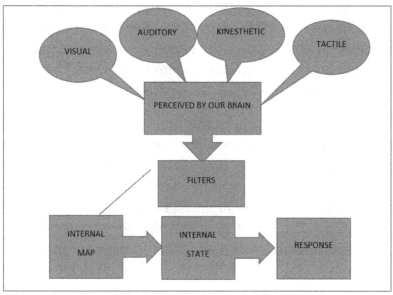

As you can see, communication starts with input. Without input, there can never be any communication taking place. Input enters the brain through the senses (sight, touch, hearing, smell, taste) and is consequently processed by the brain. The brain perceives input and filters it through experience, expectation, belief or simply mood. Once the input is filtered, the mind creates a map which then creates a state. From this, a response is created. Such a response can take the form of an answer to a question, or physical, emotional and even spiritual response.

To put things into perspective, imagine someone saying "hello". Now, this input, which is verbal, is processed by the brain and produces a response such as "hello". Seem simple enough, right? Well, what about if that person saying hello is someone you dislike? The filters in the brain perceive this input coming and may choose to produce a response in which the other party does not respond.

Now, the previous example may seem a bit extreme, but it clearly shows how filters can play a crucial role in hindering communication. Ideally, an effective communicator who possesses advanced communication skills would be able to lower these filters and elicit the desired response.

Modern life is such where the brain is flooded with input and stimuli. Think about it: television, smartphones, advertising, people, you name it. Everything around us is continuously feeding us input both at a conscious, and subconscious level. The brain will automatically process it all whether we realize it or not. And, there are times when the brain overloads. Have you tried to listen to more than one person at a time? The brain can quickly become saturated and have a hard time keeping up.

Filters can help us process weed out information which we do not deem necessary. To a certain extent, it is a defense mechanism which prevents the brain from overloading.

Generally speaking, the brain perceives input through the five senses (sight, touch, hearing, smell, taste). So, this is what the brain perceives:

- The things we see
- The things we hear
- The things we taste
- The things we touch
- The things we smell

Effective communicators can use all of these senses to convey meaning. You will often see advertisers play with these combinations to produce desired effects in potential customers. For example, food in advertising *looks* good because it *tastes* good. Or, clothes both *look* and *feel* comfortable.

In the business world, the most successful communicators combine visuals with audio to drive their message home. Great speeches make the right use of visual aids to enhance the words spoken. Religious leaders often order their followers to stand and use their hands to express worship. That is a classic kinesthetic response.

There is an adage in education: the more sense involved in learning, the easier it is for learning to take place. Great teachers differentiate themselves from regular ones by being able to use various means to drive home their message. The same holds for anyone who wants to communicate effectively.

Filters

Filters are just that: it is a selection process by which the brain organizes input. Thanks to this process, the mind can take the information it receives and interprets the message contained in the package. These filters may then interpret the message as intended by the sender, or completely change its meaning. Communication is entirely dependent on the filters of every individual. Filters are the result of the experiences, knowledge, and circumstances of our lives. For example, advertising has a completely different effect on wealthy individuals than on those who are struggling. What is the filter in this case? Your financial situation. A wealthy individual might find a new car ad appealing whereas a less wealthy individual might dismiss it entirely.

Consequently, filters can produce one of three outcomes:

- **Elimination.** The input received will be discarded since it is deemed irrelevant, or unimportant. Think of the new car ad. Will you pay attention to it if you can't afford a new car? Chances are you might dismiss it altogether.

- **Distortion.** Filter tend to alter the inputs received based on experiences and expectations. In some cases, this can lead to a complete distortion of the sender's original intent. Nevertheless, other recipients may capture the sender's real purpose. This distortion effect is different for every individual.

- **Generalization.** When a new input is similar to existing knowledge, or experience, the brain will accept it, and assign the same meaning to it as it has done in the past. This is when we say that the message "clicks". One word of caution: this new input may be deemed as similar to previous input but may actually have a completely different intent. Think of politicians who say one thing but actually mean something totally different.

In short, every person's filters will affect how the brain processes the package.

As stated earlier, filters can come from different sources: experience, expectation, circumstance, religious beliefs, political ideology – virtually anywhere. As we gain more experience in processing information, certain filters will play a more significant, or lesser, role. For example, deep religious beliefs may increase over time, whereas political ideology may shift as we age.

Some examples of filters are:

- Circumstance
- Experience
- Expectations
- Core values
- Beliefs
- Prejudice

Let's take a more in-depth look at each one of these items:

1. **Circumstance.** In essence, we all communicate differently under different circumstances. You can see this throughout the day. We communicate one way at work and another way at home. We treat colleagues and subordinates differently than family. Take the time to notice how your interactions change throughout the day according to the situations you find yourself in. By learning to recognize your environment, you will be able to put your skills to the best use possible. Your skills will allow you to make people more comfortable, adjust the level of formality, or build rapport.

2. **Experience.** What do you bring to the table every time you're in a meeting? Aside from values and beliefs, you bring experience. Experience allows you to gain an understanding of the way certain things work. This is why companies value experience so

highly in key positions. This experience has enabled you to learn from mistakes, gather information and provide examples of what works and what doesn't. Therefore, the experience will affect the way you communicate at all times. The brain uses the experience to filter inputs and determine what type of information it is. For example, if you hear someone speaking with a firm and somber tone, you might take that to mean bad news. The same goes for facial expressions.

3. **Expectations.** We all have expectations. So, what happens if inputs don't meet those expectations? For example, you're expecting to good news when you get bad news. Or, you're expecting the worst when the thing doesn't turn out to be that bad. If inputs don't match our expectations, this can lead to distortion or even elimination.

4. **Core values.** Values represent essential things in life. Our societies generally value the same things: honesty, loyalty, education, spirituality, hard work, family and so on. So, if an input goes against family, the filter might dismiss the input altogether. In the workplace, we might value our image, reputation, approval, work ethic, and innovation. These values will determine how our brains will process inputs in the workplace.

5. **Beliefs**. Beliefs differ from values in the sense that beliefs are our perception of the way the world works. For instance, we believe that hard work pays off, or that there is a higher power watching over us. Beliefs are not about what is right or wrong, or if they

are good or bad, they are our perception of what we believe if the way things are done. Thus, we can become skeptical about certain inputs if they don't line up to our beliefs.

6. **Prejudice**. Prejudice is a type of generalization. And while the word prejudice usually denotes a negative connotation, it's safe to say we all have them. Consequently, prejudice happens when we take our experience and assume that the same things will always happen under the same circumstances. Prejudice is generally the result of personal preferences and culture.

Prejudice can get in the way of communication when they represent negative ideas and feelings. For example, you think that certain people behave a certain way, or that certain ideas are bad because of X or Y reason. A common prejudice might be that people from X country are bad because they do A, B or C. Conversely, prejudice could be positive. For instance, you believe that people from country X are brilliant. That could also become misleading because if you meet someone from country X and they don't live up standards, then you might be disappointed. That is why it's so important to manage prejudice in such a way where you are always willing to test preconceived notions to avoid making false judgments.

A wise choice would be to judge individuals around you for what they are and not for what you believe they are. If you had a negative experience with a person from country X, that doesn't mean that everyone from that country is a bad person. If you do, you might be missing out on valuable and meaningful relationships which can enrich your life.

Internal Map, State, and Response

Once the entire communication process has taken place, the outcome of the brain's processing is the message extracted from the package. This outcome is what psychologists call an "internal map". This map is the way in which your brain has processed, organized and sorted information into a picture which it can make sense of. If this map is familiar and the brain can recognize it, then a certain meaning will be attached to it based on prior knowledge and experience. If this information is not recognized, then the brain must create a new map in order to assimilate this new information. This new map is often based on existing information so that it is more digestible.

It should be pointed out that new information may lead to resistance from the individual, particularly if it goes against pre-conceived notions as expressed by filters.

Once the new map has been accepted, an "internal state of being" emerges. This is the result of the map compared against filters such as expectations. For example, you hear the score of a football match. Team X has won. If this is your team, then you are happy and excited. If this isn't your team, then you might be sad and disappointed. It's the same event, but the expectations of the individual may lead to completely different states.

Once the state has been created, a response is produced. The fans of the winning team may choose to go out for dinner and have a celebration. The fans of the losing team may choose to stay home and not to do anything. This is where you, as an effective communicator, need to understand these responses. This is why effective communicators always know how to break bad news to others in the best possible way.

CHAPTER 2

———— ⋙ ————

PERCEPTION

Let's start this chapter off with a small test. What comes to mind when you see the word:

LOVE

What image does this word produce in your mind? Does it stir up positive or negative feelings? Did you picture a person? Did it evoke any memories?

For most, the word "love" evokes warm and positive feelings. For some, it may conjure up negative feelings based on painful past experiences. Whatever the response, the outcome is the product of the individual's perception. Ultimately, your way of communicating "love" will depend on your feelings, expectations, experiences, prejudice and so on.

The Perception of Our Environment

We all have a unique perception of our environment; our world, if you will. Even when two different individuals view the same event, at the exact same time, from the same angle and under the same circumstances, their perceptions of this event might be completely different. We can use our senses to "build" a perception of the world, and in turn, communicate these perceptions to others. For example, what is your definition of "love"?

The biggest tool at our disposal in communication is language. While language affords us a great deal of freedom to express our perceptions, it may also turn out to limit our ability to communicate our thoughts and perceptions. That can happen in two ways:

1. The language we use might be inadequate to express our thoughts and feelings. That is why it is common for some languages to have words that do not exist in others. For instance, "karoshi" means "to die from overwork" in Japanese. This word does not exist in the English language since it is not cultural for people to die from overwork in America. Sadly, it is commonplace in Japan.

2. The connotation given to words may differ from one person to another. Generally speaking, the word "money" has a positive connotation insofar as being the endgame of hard work. Perhaps others might give it a negative connotation since it is "the root of all evil". In any event, connotation depends on the

individual's perception as filtered through experience, knowledge, and expectations.

Consequently, language is the means through events and experience are described and communicated to other individuals. When we "map" our experiences we are offering our rendering of what actually happened. Furthermore, general truths arise from a group of individuals agreeing that an object is what it is. That is why "the sky is blue" is a general truth since most individuals agree. Anyone who disagrees may be seen as an outcast for diverging from what is considered to be generally true.

However, when we are unable to use language appropriately, four possible cases of misunderstanding may arise:

1. We tend to view language as the experience itself when it is merely a rendering of one's perception of an event which truly happened. Thus, language becomes a limiting factor since words can never truly capture the breadth of an experience. How many times have you heard someone say they are "speechless"?

2. Often, we believe that others share the same viewpoints as we do. This false assumption leads us to leave out essential bits of information from our message. This may lead to confusion or forming a false assumption of what we are really trying to convey. Skilled and experienced teachers never assume that every student knows what they are

supposed to know. Great teachers always review the basics before jumping into new content.

3. Misunderstanding can arise when you put "words into someone's mouth". That is, you make assumptions of what they are saying instead of listening to what they are actually saying. This often happens when we have known people for a long time or believe they share the same beliefs and values as we do.

4. One other crucial mistake is attempting to impose our perceptions on others. For instance, someone has lost a loved one, and you say, "I know what that's like". While that may very well be true most of the time, it can never be completely true, as each individual mourns a loss differently. Just because both of you have lost a parent, it doesn't mean that you will grieve in the same manner. This is why therapists avoid using phrases such as, "I understand what you're going through".

The Role of Language in Our Perception Dynamic

The inputs we perceive through the five senses are processed through the brain thus recreating our perception of a given event or phenomenon. In general terms, we store these perceptions as images and feelings. We choose to remember what we do because it is meaningful to us in some manner. And while we can conjure up imaginary scenarios, we ultimately internalize whatever we choose to believe or accept.

Our perception dynamic is the way in which we live in our environment. What we ultimately perceive through the senses is the way we choose to distill from each of our senses. As such, our perception dynamic is based on two core principles:

1. During our upbringing, we construct models of the world around us. Children form hypotheses of what they perceive and are eager to test them out. During this process, language becomes attached to the experiences we live. We are taught sounds and symbols which are attached to objects, events, and people. These sounds and symbols represent society's understanding of these phenomena. Along the way, we build what is known as the Auditory Digital System (ADS). This system is the way in which we talk to ourselves. This system is entirely personal and cannot be attached to anything outside of us. It is the purest form in which we perceive the world.

2. Nevertheless, we have one specific model for building our perception of the world. This is called the Primary Representation System (PRS). It is the main way in which we view the world as taught to us by society. This system acts as a filter for the language we use when communicating. This can be considered as our "default" communication system.

Research has demonstrated that the three main ways in which we communicate, from person to person, are visual, kinesthetic and auditory. Each individual has a "default" channel in which input is received. This is the way in which we feel the most comfortable to receive information. While we are able to receive information, there is always one preferred way to establish communication.

In education, these preferred channels are called "learning styles". For example, visual learners value visual input over other types of input. Auditory learners value spoken instructions over visual demonstrations. Kinesthetic learners prefer to be hands-on rather than sitting and listening to an explanation.

A good rule of thumb that you can use to identify your default channel is:

- If you need to do what you are doing, then you are most likely visually oriented.

- If you need to repeat instructions out loud while doing something, then you are most likely auditory-oriented.

- If you need hands-on, practical instructions, then you are most likely kinesthetically-oriented.

While educators have identified other learning styles, these three are the most prevalent. So, the sooner you can identify your particular style, and that of others, you can tailor your communication to suit your target audience. A good speech, presentation, talk or conversation, would incorporate elements from all three styles. This is what sets good communicators from the professionals. The most successful presentations get people moving, display engaging visuals, and use sound to convey meaning.

In any interaction you have with others, you can pick up on cues which will tell you how this person prefers to communicate. The sooner you can pick up on this, the sooner you will be able to use your advanced communication skills to reach your interlocutor and engage them successfully.

Let's have a closer look at these cues.

Verbal Cues

Verbal cues happen all the time. For instance, when you talk on the phone, you have no other input but your interlocutor's voice. The cues you get from this interaction allows you to infer meaning and decode messages based upon tone of voice, pitch, and intonation. Those who are predominantly auditory have a much easier time relating to people over the phone. They are able to figure out meaning from verbal cues just by listening.

So, when listening to another person, focus on their actual words, but also focus on their tone of voice, pitch, and intonation. This can tell you a lot more than about that person than words alone.

Visual Cues

Body language is the hallmark of visual cues. A person's facial expression, gestures and posture can speak volumes of the way they feel or even what they are thinking. Some examples of visual cues are:

- An attentive person sits up and leans forward.

- A predominantly visual person will stare at visual aid rather than the speaker.

- Auditory folks get distracted by visuals and tend to look away or even close their eyes.

- Kinesthetically-oriented people tend to fidget in their seats especially when looking at charts and diagrams.

- Visually-oriented people need to see maps, formulas, or written instructions.

One good tip to keep in mind is to "speak with your hands". This will certainly appeal to visually-oriented people as they will see your sincerity through your hands.

Auditory Cues

People who are auditory inclined will always prefer sound over visuals. Some tell-tale signs of auditory people are as follows:

- They look away from visuals.

- They move their lips while reading visuals.

- They are easily distracted by sounds.

- They can repeat and restate speech easily.

- They need music to concentrate.

- They need to talk things through, especially directions and instructions.

With auditory-inclined listeners, your tone of voice, pauses, pitch, intonation and so on, are fundamental in conveying the right feeling behind your words.

Kinesthetic Cues

Kinesthetic people cannot sit still. That simple. Some key indicators of kinesthetic individuals are as follows:

- They are always "moving".

- They are very hands on.

- They need to walk and talk.

- They need a lot of physical contacts such as shaking hands, hugging, or even high-fives.

- They constantly speak with their hands.

Kinesthetically-oriented people must always be doing something. So, asking your audience to get up once in a while, or asking your interlocutor to go for a walk while you talk will do wonders to get your message through.

Self-talk

Self-talk is an often, overlooked communication tool. By being able to talk to yourself effectively, being in touch with your feelings and perceptions, you will be able to know exactly what you want to tell others. After all, how could you communicate with others if you don't know what you want to say? This is a valuable skill that you can teach others, so they can too be aware of themselves.

Eye Contact

Eye contact is one of the most commonly-referred communication tools. Yet, eye contact is not just limited to looking at others while you are talking. Here are some cues that can tell you what others are thinking and feeling during a conversation:

- Looking up means that a person is visualizing what you are talking about.

- Looking sideways, left to right, indicates people are recalling information.

- When someone looks down to their left, they are thinking and talking to themselves.

- When someone looks down to their right, they are thinking about how they feel at that moment.

So, the next time you make eye contact with other during a conversation, these cues will give you an insight into what's going on inside their minds. This is an essential tool for an effective communicator.

Key Phrases for Eliciting Responses

Effective communicators can use key phrases to elicit the response they are looking for.
For visually-oriented people you can say something like:

If I could show you how you can profit from this venture, would you consider giving it a closer look?

For an auditory-oriented person you might say:

If I could explain to you how you can profit from this venture, would you like to hear more about it?

For a kinesthetically-oriented individual you could try:

If I could help you get a hold on this profitable venture, would you like to get a feel for it?

As you can see, by reframing the same statement you can increase the chances of getting through to your intended recipients. You are now on the right track to becoming an advanced communicator.

CHAPTER 2

RAPPORT

There is so much talk on rapport these days. But how can you separate the fluff from fact? In this chapter, we will take a deeper look at rapport and how this is one of the advanced communication skills that effective communicators exploit to get their message across.

But first, what is rapport?

Rapport can be defined as "unconscious similarity". Have you ever seen how couples who have been together for a long time seem to be "in synch" all the time? They become so comfortable with each other that they know what the other is thinking, how they will react, they have the same gestures, mannerisms and so on. This is a tell-tale sign that two people not only get along, by really like each other.

So, let's take a look at five tips which will help you master one of the most critical advanced communication skills.

Five Tips to Mastering Rapport

First off, let's look at the following diagram:

Figure 4

The Rapport Dynamic

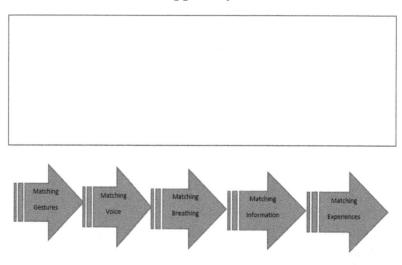

The previous chart is based on research which indicates that up to 93% of all communication is non-verbal. What that means is that your words account for only 7% of your total meaning. The remainder is made up of body language, the tone of voice, facial expressions and even breathing.

When you are trying to connect with others, bear in mind that people feel more comfortable with someone is like them. It's a lot easier to level with someone who talks, moves and even breathes, just like you.

Fear not, these tips will help you become a master at the art of rapport.

Matching gestures

To master this tip, we need to practice what we learned in chapter 3. By detecting your interlocutor's eye movement, posture, and facial expression, you can become aware of their behavior and mirror them accordingly.

So, what does it mean to "mirror" someone's behavior? Basically, it consists in mimicking their movements so that you appear to be in synch with them. For example, if your interlocutor is leaning forward when you speak, you can lean forward when they speak. But please try to avoid leaning forward when they lean forward as it would be far too obvious. If the other person crossed their legs, you can try the same. Furthermore, if they are the type of person who speaks with their hands, feel free to do the same.

Body language can be a great way of supporting another person. For example, suppose a colleague is telling about a problem they had while leaning to one side. You can lean to the same as a signal that you are on their side.

Bear in mind that there is a limit to mirroring someone's movements. For example, if you are in a meeting and one colleague has been crossing their arms and legs the whole time, then you might have to focus more on that person and see what's bothering them. This is a clear defensive posture and a signal that you might not be getting through to them.

Matching Voice

This is a great tool. You can try your best to match tone and speed throughout a conversation. If your interlocutor is a slow speaker, then you need to avoid speaking too fast. If they are a fast talker, then you might have to speed up to match their level of energy. Just be careful when someone raises their voice as you might end up in a shouting match!

Please note that when you speak with someone who has a different accent, try your best to remain neutral; the worst thing you could do in unconsciously match their accent. That's a big no-no as it might be taken the wrong way.

Matching Breathing

Breathing is a tricky one. However, great communicators who master advanced communication skills can really get through to someone. It might be hard to achieve this is you are moving around, such as walking while you talk. But whenever possible, try to inhale and exhale when your interlocutor does. This can be taken as a clear sign of support. It is a great way of building rapport as this is proof that you are "in synch".

Matching Information

This tip is more about the way you treat information rather than what information is shared.

What it doesn't mean is necessarily agreeing with someone. This tip focuses on the "size" of the information you have shared. If your colleague feels comfortable sharing small bits of information at a time, then you can try the same. The last thing you want to do is let loose a large amount of information and then expect your colleague to do the same. Perhaps your colleague is a "big-picture" kind of person and isn't interested in detail. Then you need to share information accordingly. What if your boss is very analytical and you aren't? You must try your hardest to match their level of detail so that you are on the same wavelength. It's important to avoid sharing too much, or too little.

The best course of action is to go incrementally as your interlocutor questions. This is where you can notice their style. A simple, "how are you?" can reveal so much about a person. It's important not to push people to talk as they might simply feel insecure. Great communicators get others to feel comfortable, so they can open up and share information freely.

Matching Experiences

Whenever possible, try to find something in common with your interlocutor. What could be better than kicking off a conversation by talking about things in common? This is fast an easy way to build rapport. Look for things in common such as interests, hobbies, background or acquaintances. A few, quick questions can get you started. For instance, "where are you from?" and "what do you do?" are fantastic conversation starters. You can magnify the effect of these questions by being sincere and genuinely interested in the other person. What to do if they are from a country you've never been to or don't know much? Ask them about it! If you happen to know some facts, or if someone you know has been there, share that fact, and I am sure you will hit things off.

Tools for Rapport

The tips we have discussed in this chapter are powerful tools mastered by effective communicators. Think of them as tools in the hands of a master craftsman. The craftsman may have all the knowledge, and talent and experience in the world, but without tools, he will not be able to produce much.

As you progress in your mastery of these tools, you will notice how easy and effortless it can be to become build friendships and contacts. As Dale Carnegie said, "You can make more friends in two months by becoming interested in other people than you can in two years by trying to get other people interested in you." Wise words indeed. By becoming genuinely interested in others, you will find that it is not only easier to build great relationships and lasting friendships, but it is also a rewarding experience.

Your mastery of mirroring will instantly make others feel more comfortable around you. You can ease their anxiety by making them feel like you "get them". By matching someone's tone of voice, you can indicate support without actually saying anything. You can match a tone of concern, or excitement.

Also, your mastery of eye contact will tell you exactly where people are. You can gauge whether your audience is following you, or if someone has lost interest in your presentation. By engaging others visually, you can measure their reactions.

Master communicators who use advanced communication skills as tools, can plan ahead and have a few tricks up their sleeve. For instance, you can use your voice to create an effect. You can speak loudly to get their attention, speak softly to create anticipation, or make pauses to create emphasis. Remember that your voice is the most powerful tool in your possession!

As you gain mastery of advanced communication skills, you will instinctively know what to do in just about any situation. The great thing about all of this is that anyone can learn them. All you need to do is put in the time and work needed to master these skills.

In the next section, we'll look more into an extremely powerful tool: your position of perception.

Positions of Perception

We all have a position on everything. And while your point of view is just as important as everyone else's, being able to put yourself in someone else's place is a very powerful task when trying to communicate. Master communicators are able to communicate with others at an advanced level because they are able to put themselves in the place of others.

Before getting into the three positions of perception, I'd like to make an important point: a powerful skill that master communicators learned is to not take things personally. Often, you will meet people who are rude and even aggressive. It's easy to think that it's because they don't like you. And while that could be true, there are folks who treat everyone that way.

When you learn not to take things personally and put yourself in someone else's place, you begin to realize that they are other reasons why a person is rude selfish. This point isn't meant to justify inappropriate behavior. However, when you begin to understand why difficult people act the way they do, you begin to find ways to get through to them. Granted, there are people who are best left alone. But other times, there are people who are simply misunderstood, and when given a chance, turn out to be wonderful folks.

That begin said, let's take a look at the three positions of perception:

- **First position.** This is when you see, hear and feel things for yourself. You see things with your eyes, hear things with your ears, and feel things with your own emotions. This is your experience which no one else can perceive as you do.

- **Second Position.** This is a position of empathy. You are able to put yourself in someone's place and really begin to see and feel their position on a given situation. While you may not share their values and beliefs, you come to understand the reason why they do things and the choices they have made. During this time, you stop being yourself and you become the other person.

- **Third Position.** This is commonly referred to as "third person". This is when you are a dissociated, impartial observer. Think of judge who doesn't take their feelings, beliefs, and prejudice into consideration, but is focused on the facts in an objective manner. This position puts you in the place of a spectator who is watching events unfold.

By understanding each position, you can gain valuable insights into the events taking place. You can analyze what's happening in "real time", as you interact with someone. Also, you can look back in retrospect and see what you could have done better, or differently. In addition, you'll be able to play different roles and take different sides. This ability is perfect when you are rehearsing a future interaction.

You can ask yourself the following questions:

- What do you see, feel and hear?

- What are you thinking about the situation?

- What are you thinking about yourself?

- What mental and emotional state are you in?

I invite you to take any past interaction you wish. Answer these questions and you will see how you can look at things from either the first, second, or third position. This will enable you to see what you got right, and what you could improve for next. Please remember that this is an ongoing process. The answers to these questions will tell you a lot more about yourself and your progress as a future master communicator.

CHAPTER 2

———— ✠ ————

ADVANCED COMMUNICATION SKILLS TOOLBOX

As any master craftsman, you will need to have a toolbox that can allow you to mold, sculpt and create your vision. Regardless of how talented and creative you are, if you don't have the right set of tools, it will be nearly impossible for you to produce the outcome that you truly envision.

Therefore, this chapter will focus on three specific items:

- Communicating with empathy so that others can see that you "get them".

- Move others to a deeper level of thought and break through objections.

- Guiding conversations without dominating them.

These are the best-kept secrets in advanced communication. These tools will allow you to become the master craftsman you are meant to be. After all, total mastery of advanced communication skills will allow you to improve your relationships, get ahead in the workplace and help you keep your competitive edge.

So, let's get started by taking a closer look at the advanced communication skills toolbox.

Cognitive Reframing

Cognitive reframing is a process in which you can shift the focus on a problem. In other words, it is a process in which you can transform the focus of a problem, from a negative perspective into a positive one. For instance, I always ask others around me to change the word "problem" for any one of these three: challenge, opportunity, and lesson.

When you look at problems as "opportunities", you will see how you can transform this negative situation into an opportunity for growth and development. Have you heard stories of people who started successful businesses after being fired from their jobs? It happened to Steve Jobs.
Also, problems can be the challenge. You can look at a problem as a way of using your creative power and transforming an obstacle into a solution, not just for yourself, but for those around you.

There's an old proverb which says, "if it doesn't have a solution, then it's not a problem".
In addition, problems can become powerful lessons. If you failed at something, if something didn't go as expected, then

it's a great chance to learn why it didn't work and how you can improve the next time around. Some of the world's most valuable lessons have been learned from failure. Edison eminently said, "I have not failed. I've just found 10,000 ways that won't work."

The cognitive reframing foundation is the separation of intention from behavior. While your heart might be in the right place, it's your actions that speak for themselves. Often, people make terrible mistakes despite having good intentions. Ultimately, your behavior produces consequences, and it's these consequences which can be positive or negative.

As a result, it is vital that you align your behavior with your intentions. That way, you can say what you mean, and mean what you say. Here are some examples of how you can align your intentions and your actions:

- Define words appropriately

- Set realistic timeframes

- Understand the consequences of your actions

- Realize the amount of work required in a task

- Flip problems over into opportunities, challenges and lessons

- Get the right information

- Match your intentions to realistic actions

- Change context so that your actions fit into the right circumstances.

These actions will allow you to translate your intentions into action. You can talk all you want, but at the end of the day, it's your actions that people will remember. If you talk a big game, then you best be ready to deliver. When you align your intentions and your actions, you will deliver day after day after day.

Now, let's look at an example of how you can transform a "problem" into a challenge, an opportunity or a lesson by using cognitive reframing.

For example, let's say that after you're done reading this book you have the following idea:
Mastering advanced communication skills are hard to learn.

So, how can we flip this problem around?

First, we need to define words appropriately:

- Learning doesn't involve memorization; it involves understanding and application.

- Learning something doesn't have to be hard, but it does involve some hard work.

You can also set realistic time frames:

- I will get started mastering these skills today.

45

- Every day is a new opportunity to practice and master these skills.

You also need to understand the consequences of your actions:

- I will never master advanced communication skills unless I give it a chance.

- My skills will improve if I give it my best shot.

In addition, you need to realize the amount of work needed in this task:

- Are advanced communication skills really that difficult to learn?

- Is this really the hardest thing I've ever done in my life?

Also, you must get the right information:

- Do I need more training in advanced communication skills?

- What else do I need to know?

Please remember to match your intentions to realistic actions:

- I am committed to making a serious effort.

- I am convinced that becoming a master communicator will help my career.

Finally, change the context so that your actions fit into the right circumstances:

- Do I need to make extra time for this new learning?

- Is there a mentor out there who can help me master these skills?

As you can see, asking yourself these questions will get your creative juices flowing. Often, it just takes some serious thought before you can transform a vision into a reality. Crafting a realistic plan is essential in achieving your goals. After all, "A dream without a plan is just a wish".

The use of language in advanced communication

As we mentioned earlier in this book, language is a vehicle by which you can achieve your aims. It is also a powerful tool that can be used to build rapport, get past objections and even let you guide conversations seamlessly and effortlessly.

The first thing to keep in mind is the use of "tastefully vague" language. How you can you achieve this? Let's take a look.

- **Reading minds.** This is a powerful tool. With it, you can indicate that you have "read the minds" of your audience by signaling keywords. If you get it right, you can instantly increase your rapport and easily deflect objections. You might even be able to gain agreement on the spot just by being clear in your suggestive nature. For instance:

  o You might be thinking this is hard to do, but I am sure you will get it in no time.

  o I can see how you are concerned about results, but with careful planning and supervision, the project will be a success.

  o We all agree that honesty and integrity are fundamental in the workplace.

- **Lost Performative**. This particular tool highlights a situation without indicating the source of information. It is a value judgment without indicating who is doing the judging. This action is called lost performative as you are essentially stating a fact, but not revealing where, or who, it comes from. This will allow you to guide conversations without pointing fingers at anyone. For example:

  o It's a known fact that our competitors' products are of inferior quality.

  o Those responsible for this mishap have done their best to correct the issue.

- **Causal relationships**. This goes beyond the standard cause-and-effect relationship. When you underscore the causal relationship among events, you can highlight the effects of one action versus another. This can help you skew your interlocutor's judgment toward the outcome that you desire. Also, it can help your listeners understand your point of view clearly and succinctly. For instance:

- o The bad quality of this report makes me think you don't want to be here anymore.

- o Taking an advanced communications course will allow you to improve your sales performance.

- o Your attendance to this meeting will increase our chances of closing the deal.

- **Presupposition.** A presupposition should not be confused with an assumption. An assumption is something that a person may take for granted. An assumption can stem from experience. However, a presupposition is something that you have not yet stated, but it has been implied in the language you have used. For example:

  - o We're confident that when you see the finished product, you will be thrilled with its quality (we are presupposing that the quality of our product is so good, that when you see it, you will realize just how great it is).

  - o Sales will improve as soon as the new marketing campaign is launched. (We are presupposing that the marketing campaign will be successful, and as a result, sales will automatically improve).

- **Universal Truths**. Universal truths are tough because it's not easy to achieve consensus among a large number of people. Earlier, we stated that "the sky is blue" is a universal truth because a large number of people agree that the sky is blue. You can word ideas and concepts to reflect this common agreement among large numbers of people. For instance:

  o We are all looking to make money in this deal. (We all want to make money. There is no exception because we all feel, and believe, the same thing).

  o No one wants to waste their time. (There is no person that wants to perform an action just for the sake of it. Everyone agrees that their time is valuable and wants to use it productively).

- **Tag questions**. This is a commonly-overlooked linguistic device, but it can be a powerful tool. Tag questions are commonly used to confirm information that we assume to be true. However, they can also be used to generate a consensus as you have already framed your statements in such a way that others will find it hard to disagree with you. For example:

  o The more you practice your advanced communication skills, the more you will improve them, won't you?

  o It makes sense to start saving money at a young age, doesn't it?

- **Implicit Commands**. No one likes bossy folks. But if you can tacitly give commands, then they will resonate in your interlocutor's mind in such a way that they won't even realize you are doing it. For instance:

  o Doesn't it make you feel better to have a plan? (The implicit command is "doesn't it make you feel better". You are not commanding the person to feel better just because they have a plan, but you are appealing to their sense of security as a result of having a plan).

  o I am glad to see you have decided to join us. (You are not commanding to the person to join you, but you have implied that they have made the right choice in following your command).

The tools we have described in this chapter, along with the practical tips and techniques provided in previous chapters, will enable you to stock your toolbox with a wide array of tools you can draw from in any situation. As you build your skills and gain more experience, you will come to understand how each tool may be used in a given situation. Furthermore, you will surely tailor them to suit your strengths and needs. Master communications can take these tools and add their personal touch to them.

Please bear in mind that it takes time and effort to build advanced communication skills. So, whenever you see a successful speaker, watch them, observe them, and "steal" whatever tips, techniques or tools they are using. As you gain more understanding of these skills, you will begin to recognize how master communicators play to their strengths in order to get their message across. If they can do it, so you can you!

So now that we have reached the end of this chapter, what's next? Now it's time to roll up your sleeves and make a concerted effort to practice your skills every day. Monitor every interaction you have at home, in the workplace, at the gym, at church, everywhere, and you will see just how many opportunities you have to get your message across and achieve your goals. The sky's the limit when you have mastered advanced communication skills.

CONCLUSION

———— ≋ ————

BRINGING IT ALL HOME

So, we have come to the end of *Advanced Communication Skills: Why Is It So Important to Communicate? Tips that will make you an effective communicator.* We hope it was informative and able to provide you with all of the tools you need to achieve your goals in life and at work.

The next step is the most important one: making the decision to consciously use the tool contained in this book so that you can become an effective communicator. The most important thing you need is the will and desire to achieve it. Please keep in mind that you can do anything you set your mind to.

The tool we have outlined for master communicators is the result of years of experience. The validity of these tools has been backed up by research. So, you can rest assured that we have given you a battle-tested tool. Now that you have a solid understanding of advanced communication skills, please go back and review the items which you have highlighted in this book.

I encourage you to make your plan so that you can focus on the skills that you feel you need to brush up. One great way to keep track of your progress is to keep a journal. This journal can help you chronicle your hits and misses. I recommend keeping a notebook where you can jot down important observations based on your daily interactions. Be sure to write down the date of each observation.

If you are more technologically inclined, there are several great note-taking apps which you can use on your smartphone or tablet. You can also make voice notes of your observations. This way, you can rest assured that you will keep your ideas in a safe place. Modern life can be hectic at times, so trusting technology can help you keep your head in the game.

Also, please refer back to this book as often as you need to. Master educators know that repetition is the key to successfully learning and mastering any subject. For instance, you can refer back to chapter one if you'd like to go over the fundamentals of communication. Perhaps there is something in that chapter which you'd like to share with family, friends, and colleagues.

The communication dynamic outlined in chapter two can make a great topic for a workshop or training seminar. Why not put your knowledge to good use? You can become a force multiplier and share your skills and expertise with others. That way, your team can gain a better understanding of how effective communication works. You can guide them into becoming successful communicators, too.

I also encourage you to take a long look at chapter 3 in which we discussed perception. Try to focus specifically on how you can pick out cues to determine where your interlocutors are. These cues can give you powerful insights as to whether your message is getting through, or whether you need to look into your toolbox and see what other tools can help you get your message across.

In addition, rapport, as discussed in chapter 4, is a powerful tool that you can use to build lasting relationships and get deals done. As I pointed out earlier, rapport is not easy to master, but it is worth all the hard work. When you build rapport successfully, people become comfortable around you and will let their guard down. This will allow you to get your message across while achieving your goals. This will enable you to create win-win outcomes just about every time. What could be better than that?
The advanced communication skills toolbox is our most-prized possession. This toolbox is filled with secrets that we handed down from generation to generation of a master communicator.

Through research, their effectiveness has been validated. I can also tell you from experience what they work. They do take some time to master, but when you do, you will make communication seem effortless. I guarantee that those around you will not even notice how you effectively build consensus, generate agreement and influence opinions in your favor. I am certain that the time and effort taken to master the skills in the toolbox will be worth it.

I am certain that you have what it takes to become a master communicator. Whether you have some experience with communication, or whether you are totally new, you will soon realize that advanced communication skills are the key to opening the door to great opportunities. Often, it is a question of asking the right questions to get what you really want.

Mastering advanced communication skills takes some time and effort, but the rewards far outweigh the time and effort needed to do so. You will be rewarded with better opportunities, improved relationships and a sense of accomplishment that is hard to find anywhere else. Paul J. Meyer once said, "communication, the human connection, is the key to career success". Indeed, he was right. You will soon find this to be true as your opportunities begin to exceed your expectations.

George Bernard Shaw also stated, "the single biggest problem in communication is the illusion that is has taken place". That is why advanced communication skills will allow you to ensure that there is no illusion, but rather that it is a fact. When you master the tools we have discussed, you will see just how real communication can be.

So, what are you waiting for? Get started on the road to mastery today. The time an effort you put in today will pay off in droves tomorrow. As former General and the US Secretary of State Colin Powell, one day said, "A dream doesn't become a reality through magic; it takes sweat, determination, and hard work". The man knows what he is talking about.

Since you have made it all the way here, I am sure that you have the determination to sweat and put in the hard work to master these advanced communication skills.

If you found this book useful and informative, please leave us a review on Amazon. Your comments are always appreciated!